I0518544

WHAT BOOKS PRESS

AN IMPRINT OF

THE GLASS TABLE

COLLECTIVE

LOS ANGELES

JUKEBOX

JUKEBOX

PATTY SEYBURN

WHAT
BOOKS
PRESS

LOS ANGELES

Library of Congress Cataloging-in-Publication Data

Names: Seyburn, Patty, 1962- author
Title: Jukebox / Patty Seyburn.
Description: Los Angeles : What Books Press, 2025. | Summary: "These poems
    explore the intersection between the musicality of language and musical
    references as signposts of meaning. The song lyrics and instrumental
    riffs that take up space in our brains (where arguably classic
    literature should be?) infiltrate the poems and proceed to assume a
    prominent position. They return author and reader to the moment when
    first heard and people and places associated with those moments"--
    Provided by publisher.
Identifiers: LCCN 2025030372 | ISBN 9798990014978 paperback
Subjects: LCGFT: Poetry
Classification: LCC PS3569.E88637 J85 2025
LC record available at https://lccn.loc.gov/2025030372

Cover art: Gronk, untitled, mixed media on paper, 2024
Book design by Ash Goodwin, ashgood.com

What Books Press
363 South Topanga Canyon Boulevard
Topanga, CA 90290

WHATBOOKSPRESS.COM

CONTENTS

***

And if it wasn't for the music,
I don't know what I'd do,
yeah.

Indeep

Know, at least, the sounds
That once were dear to you.

Pushkin

GATE, VANGUARD, BLUE NOTE

We eat summer cherries with cilantro and lime
and lafa (the best bread in the house),
a dip of smoked arctic char and aioli (plus dill)
and finally, a whole porgy in a cage
with wax beans and green chermoula.
We talk with the owner about the west side,
the new high line and wide bike path wending
past buildings that architects dream and I
think of my time in Chelsea with
Julie and Dimitri and all the illegal
sublets I loved for their one good feature—
a skylight, a picture window, an old stove—
how easy to find your way into the village
jazz clubs with names on album covers and listen
to whomever was playing, spending my
meager salary on the two-drink minimum—I have
not made a better investment since—

ALL THE CONVERSATIONS
I'VE EVER HAD THAT MATTERED

I know you hate Joe Jackson but can't remember your feelings for
Tom Petty. I know you hate Dire Straits but I like Mark Knopfler
plenty. You love Elvis Costello. I used to love Elvis Costello. We used
to love Roxy Music and Yaz, but now we chalk up Yaz to collegiate
immaturity. The Santa Esmeralda version of *Please Don't Let Me Be
Misunderstood* made us happy. R.E.M. was played repeatedly though
we don't know whose records those were.

You like everything with a strong guitar solo and find my affection
for pop R & B surprising. We stood on tables to dance when Chaka Khan
sang her devotion. You favor the anthemic and now attend alternative
venues because your friends are so young. I know I am supposed to like
Green Day. I told you I liked funk and you said, Red Hot Chili Peppers?
I said, no, Parliament. I went to see them on my 30th birthday for
the third time. I made James Taylor a chocolate cake for his birthday
and he and the band ate it on stage before the age of paranoia.

You only listen to classical music and think all tonal music sounds
the same. You prefer Miles Davis and Chet Baker and find John
Coltrane difficult but I told you, listening to him will make you
smarter. That song by Amy Grant is a guilty pleasure. You wanted
me to listen to MC5 as that was your criteria for attraction even though
you were a gaffer for Tom Petty. I sat by the lightboard for Phil Collins
but that didn't make the concert any better.

You had a ridiculous crush on Joe Strummer and we all thought
highly of The Clash but I was scared of the Sex Pistols.
My Hebrew teacher's son toured with Procol Harum. I have
blocked out the name of the band I saw before the taxi driver
locked the doors. We went to the Village Gate weekly,
rain or shine, one of our few smart moves. Two-drink minimum.
And the Village Vanguard and the Blue Note and when we got
home we played our albums with those names on the covers.

You thought Al Green's *Let's Stay Together* was the hottest song
ever. We could not believe Jim Croce died and knew that's how
fans must have felt when Buddy Holly, Ritchie Valens and the Big
Bopper went down in that plane. I loved *Angel from Montgomery*.
We snuck into Baker's Keyboard Lounge and they let us stay
because booths were empty. You loved Al Jarreau before he became
popular, and that terrible Michael Franks. Being able to sing all
the lyrics from *American Pie* was a badge of honor. I can.

You gave me Neil Young and Cream and I did not listen to them
so you took them back in disgust. I memorized all the lyrics
of Jesus Christ Superstar and Hair. You like Emmylou Harris.
I listened to Rickie Lee Jones with no respite. I had a thing
for Smetana and the Brandenburg Concertos. Everyone went
either to hear Yes or Billy Joel. You told me my musical taste
stopped developing when I was 17 but that is an exaggeration.
You were off by no more than six years.

You like the Foo Fighters and Big Audio Dynamite. We thought
Black Coffee in Bed was a great song and admired The Police
for mentioning Nabokov. I told you to listen to the first few
bars of Stevie Wonder's *You Haven't Done Nothin'* over
and over. We liked *Off the Wall* and that girl from the Eastern
Bloc who sang *Time and Tide*. I hated Al Stewart. You used to
imitate the Doobie Brothers. We didn't like Queen then but now
we think Freddie Mercury was some sort of alien angel.

We always liked Bowie in all his phases. We saw the guy from
the New York Dolls become Buster Poindexter and that was fine.
You dated Iggy Pop and I landed in a mosh pit where Dimitri
pulled me out and lectured me for being stupid. I was. My first
date was the Beach Boys with Larry, before Brian Wilson went
crazy and was declared a genius. We knew all the lyrics to *Brandy,*

You're a Fine Girl: "My life, my love and my lady is the sea."
We liked one-hit wonders.

We always knew Steve Albini (RIP) would do something with his
life and he did (see Nirvana, et al). We were midwestern then. I loved
Lou Reed and was surprised that I loved Lou Reed and was
surprised when I moved out west and it seemed like no one
loved Lou Reed. We were happy when he married Laurie Anderson.
You hate the Rolling Stones, claim their music all sounds the same.
You thought *Goat's Head Soup* changed everything. You despise
Joe Jackson irrationally.

You and everyone else like the first album, the acoustic
session, unplugged, less produced, more raw, more authentic,
before the synthesized layers, before the first drummer died,
before they signed with the big label, before they became corrupt,
bought out, sold out, mainstream. I listened to the radio from
the backseat of our Ford Galaxy 500 and from the backseat of our
Ford Ltd and talked through Rod Stewart's *Tonight's the Night*
so my mother wouldn't switch the station from WDRQ and still

believe it's a sign when the radio plays the right song
in the car on PCH/I-405/I-110//I-75/I-94//Woodward/The Lodge
and I always hear *Starfish and Coffee* or *Downtown* or
These Boots Are Made for Walking or *While My Guitar
Gently Weeps* or *For What It's Worth* or *Man in the Mirror*
or *Superstition* or *Flashlight* or Tom Waits' rasping
Waltzing Matilda or whatever the DJ-Deity chooses
(shout-out EZ Lee, hope you're well) just when I need it.

TONIGHT'S THE NIGHT
(GONNA BE ALRIGHT)

In the Ford LTD's banquette backseat

I listened to contraband
lyrics they
could not have understood.

I think.

                Just in case, I talked, I talked,
                expounded, informed, declared,

to block out Rod Stewart's metaphor
                for sex —

      a bird, a dove,
                something avian, something winged
                not unlike Marvell's "time's winged chariot"
as in, what are you
waiting for?

                If they found out, the radio
station WDRQ
might be turned off, but they never
        found out and
I never heard the whole
song
             only the opening

             chords before I would speak

out, to protect the free speech rights
of poor Rod Stewart, who had none

in my parent's car, not one, and he
could not have known
and it's perfectly

possible no one knew or cared

except for me, layering my voice over his raspy plea,
my parents desperate
to hear me tell them

about my life, as I am
to hear about my children's lives,
willing to turn the radio

up, down or sideways
for a small confidence, revealing some fraction
of myself, of their selves—however fragmented —

we do not even know what selves are
until
we have no access to them —

while I just
wanted Rod Stewart to sing freely
what it was all like, even if it meant I
could not listen.

ODE TO FIREFLY AND FONTELLA BASS

No one can explain why *Firefly*
went off the air when everyone I loved, loved Nathan Fillion,
$\qquad$ his wayward crew
$\qquad$ and misfit passengers:

$\qquad\qquad\qquad\qquad$ courtesan, medic, telepath, preacher. Joss
Whedon

called it "nine people
looking into the blackness of space and seeing
$\qquad$ nine different things."
$\qquad$ In their cubicles

when not shooting, the cast hummed
Rescue Me, made famous by Fontella Bass, who added
$\qquad$ *Ummm, ummm, ummm,*
$\qquad$ when she forgot the words.

$\qquad$ "Back then, you didn't stop while the tape was running."

Who does not want
what that song demands?

Firefly, I would rescue you
from the obscurity that may doom you but am suspicious
$\qquad$ that I may be
$\qquad$ a small strip of audiotape

born by being spoken into existence
(Rod Serling, season one, *The Twilight Zone*—Rod the only one allowed
$\qquad$ to use "God" in a script)
$\qquad$ a fiction myself, with little power

while our sci-fi partisans
struggle for survival in a silent sky utterly unlike ours,
                        noisy with name—nebula and neutron,
                corona and coma, filament and faculae,

                        dwarfpenumbrahaloGalileo—language to fill the void.

Rogue ship,
I recommission you, even representing only 4.7 million viewers
                        (100 billion stars in the universe)
                return to Earth-that-was,

Fontella, cradle the heavenly mic
far from the Showboat Club near Chain of Rocks, Missouri—
                don't stop, the tape
                is still running—

                        grit and shine, croon and bop, speak your mind,

                                come back for us.

IN MY ALTERNATE REALITY

My left meniscus shows no sign of weakness.
I act more than I feel
and seal my words with deeds.
No one begins a claim with "as it were"
though people use the subjunctive abundantly
since cruelty must exist
(if I could help, I would).
Pleasure has a less pretentious name
and the man playing *Ol' Man River* on steel drum
on the subway platform at 72 Street—
I remember him, I get
to tell him, I
remember you.

THE IMPORTANT PARTS

Head, shoulders, knees, toes

The first mention in *The Milwaukee Journal*, July 18, 1961: troubadour-teacher Janet Novotny, who played an accompanying accordion (making it hard to breathe from the diaphragm), traveled from playground to playground.

There is a tavern in the town.

Phrenology studies the relationships between a person's character and the skull's morphology. Austrian physicist Franz Joseph Gall (1758–1828) was the father of the science. Aristotle was the first to place mental faculties inside of the brain.

When the cop pulled me over, I cried on the shoulder of the road.

There is a ------- in the town.

We do not kneel in daily prayer. "Nor shall you install a kneeling-stone in your land, to bow down upon it" (Leviticus 26:1). Visiting Jimmy in Joliet, I kneeled when I went to Easter-mass. I ate lamb-cake. His grandmother muttered something in Polish that earned her a shushing. It did not bother me.

The most generous conjunction: *she's in love with me, and I feel fine.*

There is a ------- in the ------.

When you ride a longboard, and the tail is in the wave, you can walk, side-stepping, out to the front, and put your toes on the edge. Do it slowly, or you'll end up in the soup. Watch for men in grey suits.

I could not see the board, was diagnosed by Dr. Magder (of blessed memory) in his office, just over the Canadian border in Windsor. We took the Ambassador Bridge and sometimes, the tunnel, which threatened endlessness, each time.

------- is a ------- in the -------

.

Tommy, can you hear me? Can you feel me near you?

When a man looks at your mouth, either lean in or back away from the bar.

------- -- a ------- in the -------.

My favorite perfume blogger trumpets a brand called Herr Von Eden in slate-grey flacons, and their three new scents: Euterpe, "the pleasure giver"; Eros, the god of love, and Eclipse: absence.

Hasbro made a game called "Go to the head of the class," which has entered the rheumy realm of nostalgia.

------- -- a ------- -- the -------

.

My brother dislocated his shoulder playing basketball in high school, making the socket an unreliable home.

My daughter tore her medial collateral ligament, a band of tissue on the inside of the knee, connecting the thighbone to the bone of the lower leg.

------- -- - --------- -- the ------.

We are, in tissue and bone, broken and flawed.

The debate rages: whether eyes are soul-portals, or, infinite in extremity, toes.

------- -- - --------- -- --- -------.

MORPHO PELEIDES

blue iridescence on the wings topside
dull brown with eyespots underneath

so when it flies
it appears to appear and disappear

fan-dancing all the forest layers,
leaving the understory in search

of a mate. That's enough nature, don't you
think? Are you tired of being shown one thing

only to be told your eyes deceive you?
Myself, I don't believe

much. I don't believe

Gus Grissom blew the hatch, attacked by nerves
while waiting in the capsule for a lift

or that gentle Jimmy Hoffa survived
the brethren's deep trunk and now thrives

in the bowels of a mum nunnery—
or that belief counts more than the gods.

My god likes counting to forty (days, nights,
years), prefers his Bordeaux dry and white,

owns 40 covers of *Willow Weep for Me*
(on LP)

Bend your branches green along the stream
that runs to sea… each more mournful

than the next, in homage to the god
of blue morpho butterfly

…And there was under His feet… a paved
work of sapphire stone… Who taught who

to come and go as if not needed here?
Though we get how vision works (hail retina!

hail assembling brain!) that remains unclear.

ODE TO SIMULTANEITY

Scott Joplin died in a mental institution
       the year my father was born in Toronto,
the final card in his parents' hand, almost
       enough for a game of gin. King of ragtime,
Joplin suffered a breakdown when his
       opus work, *Treemonisha,* met with no
success. Another genius depressive,
       Rachmaninoff, felt stifled by being asked
to play *Prelude in C# Minor* at every
       concert. He died in Los Angeles, after
a period of relative unproductivity and
       Slavic melancholy—a description of tone,
not a diagnosis—the year my parents
       married in the rabbi's study in Detroit
before they boarded trains to Edmonton,
       Alberta, where my father served in the war,
flying cargo planes to Alaska. Abraham
       Maslow, famed psychologist known best
for his Hierarchy of Needs, developed
       the concept of self-actualization, leading
to that of cognitive dissonance and
       the study of motivation. What makes one
proceed in the face of suffering, misery?
       Compared with these men, my parents
lived small lives that wove through great
       moments of inspiration and creation,
but here I am, suturing them all together
       with the sturdy twine of the 21th century —
how time unifies the disparate, how time
       loves us, and love, as Thackeray said, makes
              fools of us all.

A LITTLE BIT OF *THE MOLDAU*
BY SMETANA

> *The connections, the connections, the connections.*
> Charles Eames

The dynamics *allegro commodo non agitato* indicate a fast
though leisurely tempo without restlessness

or agitation—swirling flutes imitating tributaries
and mermaids, twists and turns of the Moldau,

the great Bohemian river, before the melody begins,
which sounds like the Israeli national anthem, *Hatikvah.*

Smetana's symphonic poem an adaptation
of a previous composition, *La Montovana,*

circa 1600—inspiring *The Little Owl Got Married* (Slovenia)
and *The Ox-Driven Cart,* (Romania), which composer

Samuel Cohen used when he set the anthem's poem,
"The Hope" by Napthali Herz Imber, a poet from Zolochiv,

then Austria-Poland, a town nicknamed "The City of Poets."
Stan Getz adapted the tune and called it *Dear Old Stockholm,*

then recorded by Miles Davis and John Coltrane—
you should hear it on saxophone with a backbeat—

hope in those rising scales that counters the rueful
E minor. My mother could conjure up the words

to *Mean to Me* long after she forgot my name—
if my memory goes, you may have to remind me

that I did not compose *The Moldau* and am not
Bohemian, though relieved I did not imagine

the connections. I used to hear what sounded
like shards of symphonic pieces in my head,

some phrase or riff had lodged there, but now
I think that's just the noise of the brain trying

so hard, sorting and disposing, sifting, compiling,
and if the cerebellum's gears make music

from my mental mayhem, all the better.

WEATHER IN THE OC

Today, say "every" with all three syllables,
the way KISS did in a rock' n' roll anthem.
Thank The Police for citing Nabokov
in their paean to inappropriate infatuation
and don't think them pretentious bastards.

The way a child surrenders full weight
to a shoulder: how you felt this morning,
briefly, before dawn knocked. Cue: details.
Apologies, apologize: today's task.
Every day's task. The trick: to keep from
needing to make amends. Your new pen,
a fine-point Pilot, says: you hold me wrong.

If you keep plucking fruit from the tree
of contrition, you will bankrupt yourself
of remorse. Someday you will try durian,
the Thai king of fruits. Some say it smells
sweet: others, like turpentine and sewage.
Its thorn-covered husk thwarts amateurs.
Take it as your mascot: not to everyone's taste.

Nominations for the homecoming court
closed at 11:59, Eastern Standard Time.
You read the fine print. No one else did.
You will be queen and her attendants,
a lonely multitude in tulle. Abject; abdicate.
You can keep your domain name, though
it's filled with someone else's content.

If contentment meant more, ambition
would take the back seat, still depressing

an imaginary brake pedal when it felt
you came too close to the bumper ahead.
Let me drive, you said: your third wish.

THE NEARLY

impossible to ruin—certain songs—*Fever*, recorded
by Little Willie John, covered by Miss Peggy Lee—both
versions envision environs fiery with a nearly
impossible-to-sate state of desire.

Willie didn't like it, but went along—an ominous
arrangement with finger-snapping, "marginally lightened
the mood"—moans, minor-key with low saxophones, jazz guitar.
Peggy's turn torched, only bass, drums and snaps—

she subbed in history—Juliet and Pocahontas
brought their best beaus, centuries of sultry, continental
innuendo. More took up the gauntlet—The Cramps, Elvis,
La Lupe, none bad, none of them Willie's

original—anything can be ruined, or damaged,
or diminished (says Frost and his mid-wood bird)
even what you were given
to remember by those bossy muses

of recall—a student-body president's speech, an unsigned
charcoal sketch of a barn, a faintly military jacket
with matching slacks. Whatever your task, be unwavering,
Fahrenheit and centigrade, speed-dial

the DJ—she's lonely in a dark room fireflied with odd
bits of neon, with knobs, buttons, the most compact of discs,
LPs and cassettes that testify to all she has missed—
I have been her, awaiting your request.

BRIGHT SIDE

With a Roud Folk Song Number #19526,
you would not imagine
        such familiarity
but even in days of discord, when "days"
are not days but vague
        clumps of time,
every person is born on one of them —
the explanation for knowing
        this thin rhyme.
The problem-child, Wednesday, originally
Friday, which, to distance
        from the crucifixion,
lobbied with success for the switch, Wednesday
asleep at the wheel,
        and Thursday, with far
to go (a compliment, of sorts) was once Saturday,
either working hard for
        a living or loving, giving.
So goes Wednesday, hump-day, full of woe,
though weekly studies show
        this population
manages to find meaning, make car payments,
despite the bad luck chronicled
        by a Victorian
fortune-telling ditty, and most of those polled
(high response rate) still have
        their original nose.

WILD ONE

Dimitri threw his arm into the crowd
I'd fallen under, bodies bowed against
each other, bouncing back like rubber bands
as though we were elastic. We were not.
I was Eurydice, my brief descent
into the underworld aborted by
my friend, who watched me, standing on the fringe
at Iggy Pop, playing in West Chelsea
before that part of town was spic' n' span.
Or wait—was I Persephone, abducted by
the mosh pit's joyful violence. Once out
I found a beer. I couldn't think—which girl
had eaten pomegranate seeds and had
to stay in Hades half the year? I licked
a little blood off my teeth. A guy flicked
ashes on my shoes. This was before tattoos.
The bodies slammed. I'd had enough damage.

RIDDLE ME THIS

I will not wait in the egg line today
It winds around the kefir and hummus stand
past the fishmonger who
sells me white sea bass and trout
There is heirloom cauliflower and napa cabbage
blood oranges to sample
and mushrooms from outer space
sold by a lovely couple who
really know their fungi
But I will not wait in the egg line today
Three sides of a giant square
It's Beach Boys T-bird weather and I
forgot my new bucket hat
but my sunglasses are fake Chanel
and I look hot in
and through them There's a guitar
player and I ask for *In the beginning* by
Emerson, Lake & Palmer and
give him a pluot and he laughs and plays
the introduction before veering
into *Blackbird* which I also would have
bartered for but I will not wait
in the egg line today
though they have duck and quail eggs, too,
and the insides of the
brown are wonderfully, weirdly orange
sunset orange Oh this
gorgeous world The sky is scramble
and fry and nobody dances
sober said My buddy Cicero my favorite
Roman skeptic

MOLLY PICON MOMENT

Our rabbi emeritus commented on Bach and Steely Dan,
and I said, wanting him to know I had been listening
all those high holy day sermons, *I thought you were more
of a Goat's Head Soup guy*, which I also could have said
to my former teacher, for whom I feel similar reverence
and was pleased I had the gumption (*chutzpah*, yes)
to say anything to him at all. Anything. He was pleased.
Well, yes, that's true. Score one for the congregant.
My teacher and his wife took me to their favorite fish
restaurant in Los Alamitos, and we had a lovely time.
Relationships change, though I cannot imagine greater
intimacy with the *rebbe* than that moment when I said,
I remember something about you that you said to all
of us, and used it to make a connection between myself
and you. I know we should not revere people—a strange
word, from Latin for fear, to stand in awe of, so perhaps
it is not quite right, here, (fear and awe already have
a marker on them) but I would not mind others wanting
from me a certain quality of respect, and my students
probably get a little scared when I rant on about words.
I have listened to *Goat's Head Soup*, which some critics
loved and some hated, recorded in Jamaica because
Keith Richards had been kicked out of nine countries
and was bored with Switzerland. Indulgent and moody,
dark, just the sort of music a rabbi and poet might like
and I have said more than once, Mick Jagger is probably
the sexiest man in the world, which distances him from
the men discussed here, but I imagine the three of them
could have a solid conversation, and for various reasons
I would be silent but pleased, having made such a *shidduch*.

GAMES THAT HELP ME SLEEP

I almost made laudanum on Words With Friends
and found retina on Ruzzle, so have decided
to take a cheat day from my diet of doubt,
my stringent regimen of dwelling on trouble,
my abiding attraction to, affection for anxiety.
I will say, I am not lonely. We are a robust group
with a detailed charter, strategic plan and many
vice presidents but I need a new crowd.
Hope poured me three fingers of Irish whiskey
which does not make me regret like Scotch
and I am going to drink it down at that bar
on the tip of the peninsula where aging surfers
talk about the one, the wave, that got away.
Is it depth that makes the Pacific, pacific?
On nights where it gets prematurely dark,
I go in search of my lost intention, try to
Make your ears hear what your mouth utters.
On the jukebox, someone punches Dick Dale.
Last call. Just give me something salvific
so I can stop redecorating the clubhouse.

BABY, IT'S COLD OUTSIDE

Every morning I check in with Humptulips
a town of 216
in the great state of Washington
and review the state of the snow
on the Snoqualmie Pass
where chains are required except
on all-wheel drive.

My favorite weathergirl is Brittany Boyer
who is wearing a nice red turtleneck
and currently focusing on the southeast —
storms, with sunglasses in Jacksonville.
How much we can know now —
is it any wonder there is no room
for Proust in my brain?

Avalanche warning around Mount Hood
with an unstable snow cap.
Santa Ana winds on our frontier
here in SoCal—stock up on tissue.
Myself, I rely on Dolbear's Law
which equates a rise in temperature
with an increase in a cricket's chirps:

count the number of chirps in 15 seconds,
add 37, and there's the temperature
in Fahrenheit, named for Dutchman
Daniel Gabriel Fahrenheit, in 1724.
He also determined the body's temperature
to be roughly 96 degrees.
God, I love information, thank you

for information, the Information Age.
Imagine me centuries ago, mumbling
"Make me oh Lord, thy spinning wheel complete"
then getting whacked about the head
for daydreaming during
the tasks appointed me
perhaps having a prescient Peggy Lee moment,

"Is that all there is?"
while my mother,
17th century Shirley, wise beyond
her century, listened
to the crickets and threw
more wood on the fire.

SHIP OF THESEUS

Whether the ship is still
        the original ship
If most or all of its
            parts have been replaced
seems to have no human
    application

So I am struggling to care about this barque

this "thought experiment"

that so entranced
        Heraclitis and Plato and Plutarch

I do not travel
    with a terribly philosophical

crowd, have whittled my circle
        down to four friends
none of whom
        own small boats

We do not talk about odd
        abstract notions
but twice of late
    someone has mentioned this strange

ship, so I must "ponder"
        like the famed Greeks,

the issue of when
    something is no longer

its authentic
                    Self. I have not

been myself for quite some
                                time—this mood and mole
I do not recognize,
this
            constellation of spots across
            my knuckles,
                    all these nautical cap-

sleeve shirts—who
            bought them?

I am not immune to looking
                    deeply, to leaning over
the edge
of   a well, I see

cubist Ozymandias in boulders, Greta
            Garbo in ice floes

I can make
                    a connection between
euphoria and euphony beyond

                            an obvious root—the "eu"
                            ancient Greek for "well"

though the latter traveled
                    through France
and the former implied a state of joy

                    drug-induced —
not sure I have

            the lungs to chase down
            this poem, this "thought experiment"—I am
a practical girl from a practical town

who likes
            pretty music with a dollop of Stravinsky

thrown in—I trained myself
                    to like John Coltrane and now

the riffs are all I know that
            make sense
                        of this and I'll buy you a beer

AS FOR THIS WHOLE
MATTER OF HAPPINESS

The sweetest sounds I'll ever hear are those inside my head.

Richard Rodgers

That night, I kept
losing things.

   She performed Judy
Garland, my dad's favorite,
     to a room lit by
caged fireflies in rows.

That day, at the school fair, I learned
about
Rosa Parks and Alexander the Great
Information everywhere
If only the sun did not ask
so many questions.

You hear
the bass player
    when he takes a solo, fingers
      snap and flatten strings on
       the fingerboard

  hummingbird horizontal hovering

and when you stop
listening for him

  (like a west village bar you
can find only when drunk).

         The line   belonged
to a musical, "No Strings," written
in 1962, at January's close

Rodgers after Hammerstein's death

and opened   at the Fisher Theater
in downtown Detroit, where I
         was born.

On Broadway, Diahann Carroll played
the female lead to Richard Kiley's leading man.

Carroll: Black. Kiley: white.
                         The script did not
comment.

             The musical theme
borrowed from generous Johannes Brahms,
Piano Concerto #2.
         There is nothing original.

The day laden
                 with American history:
         Teddy and Franklin,
         Dred Scott, Scottsboro.

                  How
did you think of this subject?
What are you most proud of?
                  The bass's lowest pitch within
         an octave of the lowest

frequency the human ear can detect
distinctly

Listen for it

I will never be
a jazz crooner, I will never play
the upright bass,
I told my father, nearly
30 years dead.   He said:

I have news for you.
You will not   complete your tasks or fulfill
your dreams, and I said,

I will never
see you again, and he said
inside my head, I know
that, too.

I found
my pearl-drop earring, my parking stub,
my reading glasses' case minus the glasses

they are looking elsewhere

while her voice, languorous, lingered
over history, dips and runs, melisma and odd
vibrato nudged us
forward into night's
phrase and riff —

progress, of sorts.

EPISTLE TO PYTHAGORAS

You'll have to forgive me, I can't quite hear
what with the neighbors' electric scooters
and metal runes, much music of any sphere
these days, though I fear age the problem's root.

A girl's minimal t-shirt declared
"If it's too loud, you're too old." Pithy truth.
When young, in odd moments, symphonic shards
would travel my ear (not to sound so couth),

vestigial memory of being
Mozart's second flute or the concertmaster's
idiot daughter listening from the wings.
Now losing sounds both farther and faster,

days more digital and less audible,
my fears and losses, bad company, reap
and sow, while the mild rain, laudable
for growing things, will not let me sleep.

WHAT I'M REALLY SORRY FOR

I lit off loud, luminous fireworks that probably
traumatized your pug and standard poodle
(an interior room and treats, recommended)/

I told my son that your son is a whiner/

I rolled my eyes at my husband's inability
to hear me while I am facing away/

I order unnecessary shoes online in lieu
of reading balanced commentary/

I apply overpriced serum to my nascent jowls
serum that translated back into money
could feed a lean child for months/

I sent away the old random vases though
they have served the purpose of their
flower-bosses/

I have delayed/

I have been afraid of others who wish me
no harm/

I wished the owl loitering nearby
with his baritone
away/

I have frayed relations with those who
wish me well by my indifference/

I have judged
the squirrel who tightropes
my back wall to eat my figs/

the SUV that just avoided hitting the squirrel,
the driver's carelessness, her motives when
all she wants is—well, how do I know what
she wants, I impugn her carbon footprint
while luxuriating in mine/

I pretend to see into the soul of things
and understand their careenings/

I forgive actual violence but not
the metaphor (I am okay with that)/

I act as jury, being so conflicted with various
voices in my head that leave me unable to
commit to a path/

I submit to small fits of wrath, assert
if I am not for me, who will be?/

and plead rhetorical questions on the approaching
Day of Atonement (once over, it's always approaching)/

I smugly sing every verse of the closing song
Adon Olam or Ein Keloheinu (they are boring)/

I am flat and sharp/

for all of the above, I must make amends with
the individuals affronted, slighted, singed,
ignored, derided, defied, dismissed, denied/

this could take me all year, what with my
work, my family and friends, their numinous
expectations, my paltry stabs at progress/

can we get an early start, my calendar of
contrition already filling up/

it should leave me little time this year
to botch and blunder, to err, ruin, spoil and mar/

but I will find a way/

EVERYTHING THAT EXISTS ON DRY LAND ALSO EXISTS IN THE SEA, EXCEPT THE WEASEL

Talmud, Chullin 127

In my next life, I shall be a weasel.

A kolinski—Siberian—valued for its fur, its tall hair used to make paintbrushes.

If not a kolinski, then a least weasel, the smallest living carnivore.

I received a letter from my furrier—did you know I had a furrier?—asking me
to register a protest against a new California law banning the sale of fur.

My mother's mink coat with the ermine collar lives at the furrier in Tustin. Inland.

The least weasel sounds diminutive but has big plans. The males twice
the size of females. They mate often and are entirely unhelpful with
their offspring.

As you see, I am making some changes. I plan to be a predator and not too picky.

In my head these days, the famous song about us weasels: Roud Folk Song 5249. Roud is
a database of 25,000 folk songs collected from the English tradition. Compiled by Steve
Roud.

If I can't be a weasel, I will indenture myself to Roud.

No one really knows what the title/refrain means. Many speculate: the weasel
could be a tailor's flatiron, a hatter's tool, an actual dead weasel, a piece of silver
plate,

or a spinner's weasel, a mechanical measuring device six feet in circumference:
40 revolutions produce 80 yards of yarn: a skein.

A popping sound after the 40th revolution.

"That's the way the money goes"—part of the lyrics in most versions—could refer to pawning one's coat for food or drink.

The song originated in 1825 and again in 1852—we don't really know—and became a popular dance in the royal court that trickled down to the stage to dance halls to barrel organs to a children's game not unlike

Musical chairs.

I hate musical chairs. In the same family as Red Rover, which is probably one of the 62 reasons I should be in therapy.

As a weasel, therapy will not be an option. Nor will there be something analogous to me living in the sea.

No marine counterpart.

I will be lean and unaccountable.

ON 72: THE BROADWAY
SATELLITE STATION

From *Wildcat*, a song with words I still know:
Hey, Look Me Over, because my brothers sang it
in a high school musical while I was in the crib.
Ol' Man River, from *Showboat*, sung by Paul Robeson—
Kern and Hammerstein wrote the song with him
in mind. A snippit of *Jesus Christ Superstar*,
(a cast album I have memorized) and *Steam Heat*
from *The Pajama Game* began when I pulled
into the driveway. And so I stayed in the car.
Optimism, strength in the face of despair, faith,
and sex. For those who can enter the heart
of another through the strange vehicle
of notes—I do, I will, I love you.

SONG OF THE INFIELD

"These are the saddest of possible words…"
Franklin Adams

I sing of three young men
from Chicago: Tinker, Evers, and Chance—
famed for double-plays that blended

metaphor and lore—a young boy chants
their galloping names until the stands
are full of rhythm: *Tinker to Evers to Chance.*

I sing of a boy in 1907—let's hand
the kid a miracle—though he might outlast
two great wars and watch a man land

on the moon, he'd not forget the fast-
ball pitch, the hit that found its way
to Tinker's mitt, then Chance's glove and blasted

off to second's Evers—one more day
of Giant-killing en route to the gonfalon—
hidden in dactylic chorus, sound display

of making myth that lingers on
as myths will do, long after all of them and us—
the boy, too—are gone.

CUATRO PREGUNTAS:
PASSOVER IN SPAIN

In Palamos, Catalonia, why do I remodel
          the purpose of night?
Is the castle atop MontGrí another unfinished Gaudi?
       Why oh why oh why oh

      Your mother retired here
with her sister. They made the decision after the latter
            died (the other already gone ten years)
because the only Spanish they knew

were the words to *Besame Mucho,*
          a big hit when they met their soon-to-be
G.I. husbands in 1941.
      Why is this night, on this night, do we?

      The matzah lacks flavor,
compensates in texture. The condiments bitter
         and made moreso.
We recline as a sign of liberty

(someone obliged to say, are we really free? Others sigh.)
          and the mystery glass evaporates.
The door held open by a water bottle.
      Anyone could have wandered in and downed

      the prophet's portion, but I was sitting there
the entire time, and saw no one
         cradle the bell.
My daughter: where does it go? I shrug.

All that happens way after tonight's vital, viral story
          retold with Q & A, its songs of accrual,

its harried symbol: Lo, this
　　　　is the bread of affliction.

　　　　We sing about a kid—a goat—an only kid,
and another song that refrains,
　　　　　　　"it would have been enough"
as hunger grows and wanes.

If you want to visit the old
　　　　　　　Jewish quarter in Barcelona,
don't blink. You would. Look here:
　　　　Shirley and Marilyn in the marketplace,

　　　　　　　　　　　making faces at all that ham.

DAWN 101

1.
Every morning I listen for an idea
after a search for apparitions

(they have three conditions)/
I interrupt: give me three wishes.

We are not genies, they say,
We are the locals: *genius loci.*

2.
Every morning one idea that will sit
in the backseat

and fiddle with the radio until a song
that gives me a sign comes on.

I look for trouble, the rubble of dream.
It's a merge, I say, maybe my last words.

3.
See that old so-and-so humming (as we do)
to himself? I saw him walk slowly

across the street, and for once was patient,
thought he might be an angel here to test

my hospitality—let me not fail
on something so obvious

NOCTURNE: RIFFS

Each night at midnight, a northern wind
finds the bedroom window and strikes
the harp's strings to awaken King David.

He calls God, "midnight."

Chopin wrote 21 of them. Ignace Leybach
remembered only for his fifth. Fauré, Scriabin,
Satie, Poulenc. Debussy. Shostakovich. Mendelssohn.

Have a secure grasp of the long phrases.

Whistler painted a series in a veil of light.
Quoth John Ruskin: "asking two hundred guineas
for flinging a pot of paint in the public's face."

Ruskin: the only child of first cousins.

The test pattern was often a card at which
the television camera pointed while the transmitter
was active but no program was being broadcasted.

Replaced by static and snow.

In "Midnight," a movie made in 1939
(screenplay co-written by Billy Wilder)
Claudette Colbert played "Baroness Czerny."

The Times said: "three cheers and a tiger."

If there is the whole day about you, how
fortunate you are. If there is the whole dark
about you, you have until dawn to convince

the night-blooming cereus to thrive.

I WAS TALKING TO YOU

This goes out, I used to say, though
my listeners were few—devoted—
        few—on my Tuesday jazz show, 4-8
        p.m.—I came from work, left
early—cramps, I'd say, my boss
would roll his eyes—it was
            a summer job and I was under-
            qualified, did not speak
French well enough to argue
with our vendors—rode
        my Huffy from Evanston to
        Skokie, back, wiped off and re-
deoderized when I arrived
at Studio A two minutes shy
            of the hour when someone had
            to say, it's 4 p.m. at WNUR,
Evanston, Chicago—I'd play
a track that lasted eleven minutes,
      "Mediterranean Sundance" from
      Friday Night in San Francisco,
three guitarists—McLaughlin,
Di Meola, De Lucia—all I have
            forgotten why do I remember
            them—and while they jammed
I'd grab another dozen records,
pot up one half a rotation back,
      (as one song fades you turn
      the volume on the other up)
and sit and breathe—
a side of *Kind of Blue*
           a side of *Time Out*—
           one day, a *Take the A Train*

marathon, another only Ella,
Sarah, Carmen—I treasured
            my themes and never heard
            that listeners didn't—were there
listeners? Friends would call
and say, are you alive? My voice
                        would get a little low, it was
                        the airwaves, maybe, or my
unintentional persona—that's
how lower case gods talk, we don't—
            have much power but our
            voices come from nowhere—
travel to where we are not,
all pitch and tone—we speak
                        to everyone and no one,
                        less than—the music,
adjacent to the music—we
prefer to be overheard.

PASSWORD QUESTIONS

Pressed for answers, I claimed my favorite song
The Waters of March by Antonio Carlos Jobim,
my favorite store Coast Philatelics, as I admire
the perspicacity of stamps, my favorite part
of Michelangelo's David his wrists and ankles,
my favorite bird the white spectacled bulbul
(from Hindi for nightingale) and my favorite marble
Cipollino, in which you can see the onion's layers,
white-green with wavy green ribs, something about
strata and something else about mica. My favorite
metaphor, "the carnage of roast beets"—I do love
beets, the taste of dirt—we eat nine pounds a year—
and so/too much? beauty. I am a sucker for beauty.

There is a singer everyone has heard,
Loud, a mid-summer and a mid-wood bird....

Robert Frost

WHAT FLAUBERT SAID

Stay away from stonefish
(they are ugly and deadly)
and sleep like the snail for three years.
If you need a substitute fingerprint,
consult with the koala.
For parenting lessons, consider the pigeon.
The barn owl is prone to divorce
and the male ends up with a less-attractive partner.
You can envy the axolotl
its ability to grow new body parts
but the real winner, the *Turritopsis dohrnii*,
is immortal, transforming from
its medusa form back into polyps
when threatened. *There is not a particle*
of life that does not have
poetry in it.

SOME DAYS IT'S HARD
TO FIND A PURPOSE

I chased a flocculent sky into a chain-link fence,
and exchanged a few sentences
with an unexpected friend.
Our winter winds have abated
and I can tell the world awaits
my position on gratitude: it's a nice theory, but I am
a pragmatist, a lousy liar, often distressed
by the edges of day, when I expect
too much or am discontent with the little
progress made. Maybe thirty birds on a wire—three wires—
three birds on the lowest. Silhouettes. Are they mindful,
or lonely? I like to trap myself
in cul-de-sacs where I rarely belong to witness
the clouds' dispersion. Firmamental auction:
opaque, pointillist, gone. Crowds are often
told to disperse—there is danger
in numbers, in wholeness, in beauty—
the world to come is a place where they
exist, and we may want that,
but must be content with this.

AGAINST *WELTSCHMERZ*

Today I am relying on the 7 Greeks for solace.
The 7 Greeks, and leftovers: broccoli, soggy
chopped salad, and half an avocado. A serpentine
gesture of olive oil and three drips of soy sauce.
Archilochos is a favorite. And I think
Diogenes and I would have spent many hours
at Sid's bar on old Newport Boulevard, in Costa
Mesa, before pest inspectors rightly closed it.
"I have come to debase the coinage," he wrote.
If you do not find that funny, we probably
have no basis for friendship. That is not a threat.
I am not the only friend out there, and we each
offer a different range of trills and bird-songs.
You know I am fond of the common loon.
Its eerie aria not for everyone. Archilochos
disapproves of Thracian up-dos and claims
the fox's eleventythree tricks don't compare
with the hedgehog's one trick. I like hedgehogs,
the Greeks and leftovers. On this day,
I believe the world-weariness will fade,
much as dew fades. I am also fond of dew,
how it is reliable and ephemeral, all at once.

CROWS, EXPLAINED

I believe the two crows on my lawn
are lesser gods
transformed by an infraction of the Greek honor code:
being inhospitable
or committing patricide, fratricide, matricide
(affix clearly the issue)
are punishable offenses.
I believe their names are Horace and Esme,
Zelda and Bob.
I believe their names are Otto and Ada
like good palindromes, living
backwards and forwards.
For this, they had to pay.
Life is a transaction.

They are social and mate for life,
my crows, so they brook
no jealousy, no breach, no
betrayal. They do not tire
of one another. They do not
trade up or down for looks, money, age.

My crows are American crows
not the common raven or rook, not the fish
or carrion crow.
They do not hunch their shoulders.
Their name from, of course, the ancient Greek
for "short-billed." They are smart, self-
aware, even tolerant.
They recognize individual faces and if
they don't like yours, they tell their friends.
Yes, they travel in a murder.

Not an ostentation, a parliament, a knot, a skulk.
One folktale claims they gather to decide
the fate of another crow.

TODAY'S FLUTTER OF QUESTIONS

I know that the sparrows are
not talking to me. Their speech
seems to favor a few key
phrases: found food, found shelter,
predator alert. Torture
that worm. Good work on that nest.
Are there arguments? Gossip?
Kvetching? Prayer? Praise? Discourse on
existence? Vacation plans?
Are some birds more voluble
than others? Snow White spoke-sang
to bluebirds. St. Francis preached
to a literal flock, "clothed
in feathers." Aidel, daughter
of the Baal Shem Tov, also
conversed with avian friends.
Silence. Birds, where did you go?
I liked eavesdropping on you.

SWALLOW (HIRUNDO)

Barn, red-chested, Angolan,
pacific, hill, welcome, white-
throated, Ethiopian,
wire-tailed, blue, white-bibbed, pied-
winged, white-tailed, black and rufous,
pearl-breasted. Names should not
exceed four syllables with
or without hyphens, the word
"island" shall be limited.
Modifiers are everything.
The committee is neutral
on patronyms—there are ten
guiding principles for bird
names. Swallows do fine until
you consult the master list,
and then, who would not elect
the Cream-eyed Bulbul, Crescent-
Caped Lophorina or her
friend, Lesser Lophorina?

I COULD TALK ALL DAY
ABOUT THE MAGPIES

The Eurasian version one of the few
non-mammals to recognize itself in the mirror.

Pica Pica, they are also fine singers and Rossini
named an opera after them, *The Thieving Magpie*,

where he impugned their character, though they
are not drawn to shiny things, as suggested. The ones

we saw at the vineyard in Paso Robles, *Pica Nuttali*,
had distinctly yellow bills, so they may not know

who they are, given the chance at reflection.
Eurasian magpies may have neophobia:

(fear of the new) while our Central Coast American
magpies seemed comfortable near us, amidst the rows

of vines, atop a pole wearing a small sign:
Cabernet Franc, to identify the grape.

Jet black, bright white and yellow, comely avians,
the species has its own rhyme assigning joys

and traumas to different numbers. Seven for
the devil or secrets, depending on the century.

I believe we saw three, which in the 1800s meant
a funeral, though maybe we saw the same two,

which is mirth, a word I love because it doesn't sound
happy. Since the magpie knows it exists, does it understand

happiness? Do you? Thoreau believed it would come
and sit on your shoulder if you did not seek it.

TIME CERTAIN

I have descended into burial cities
and stepped in a furtive fashion

to avoid skull water, fallen for
taleteller, upstream, crewcut

(always the compound fellows),
marveled at the minute knots

tied between each pearl (tested
against my thinning front tooth),

purchased a Turban Squash,
an Oca, a head of Romanesco

with its Fibonacci pattern, sliced
and diced a Salsify and Samphire,

chewed on many a grooved ferrule,
pinched my purlicue to rid myself

of the tenanted ache in my temples,
fed the birds (tuppence a bag)

(Poppins' persistent pigeons), asked for what
I desire, pretended I do not desire,

turned "desire" into a *jamais vu*
with a bad case of semantic satiation,

collected box tents and agraffes—enough
liquid stars and pies for a lifetime.

What have you done? (Accusation?
Inquiry?) I have 99 problems.

For and on the record (think LP)
you, spontaneous and calendared,

in short-term and long-run, you
my closing bracket, parsing my space

into deserving parts of speech,
my gem, my toothsome parsley

stem, are not even one of them.

FRACTURED HERO'S JOURNEY

We went on a 12-sparrow walk

so I could teach my soul to speak.
        (Jim Harrison said this
                is the language of poetry.)

(Few things scare me as much as the word "soul.")

We climb No-Name Trail until the coastal ridge
        in some silence,
                to give our hearts their full retinue

and because we have run out of things to say.

I do not look back like my favorites
        from ancient tales. We climb
                down before we climb   up—

whether you prefer to begin with hill or speed

says as much about you as the test
        that showed I perceived and judged
                in equal measure.

Measured, measured   and found wanting.

No balladeer will record these sagas, lined
        in artichoke thistle
                and prickly pear cactus   a little poison oak

and we don't lie

to the tourists who ask, almost there?
        They may be confused angels.
                We point them toward horizon

which shares nearly everything with orison,

an ancient word for prayer
        I find hard to

                    (and therefore do not) pronounce.

MY POCKETBOOK

My 20%-off online offer is waiting.
It says: there are no restrictions.

What I really want is a juicer
another season of "Firefly"
a bird named Eleanora Cockatoo
who squawks "Eleanor Rigby"
Purple-martin houses and pink, flocked trees.

I switch to match, or out of boredom
leave a penny in each handbag.
One bivalve-shaped. One envelope clutch.
One black velvet pillbox.
Each with a coin purse, a mirror.

Each year at services, Ellen Cervantes
(I asked someone her name) wears
an excellent hat: a bow cloche, a satin
pillbox, a sheer-brimmed lampshade,
a visage boater, a fascinator, a giselle.

I can't wait for Yom Kippur this year
when we rehearse our own death

COINCIDENCE

Anything in Latin sounds profound.

In the future-perfect, wearing tunics
and driving hovercrafts, no one will utter
phrases like "there is no I in..."
though wheel of fortune sages
claim the "e" most utilized
on the visual stage.
Apparently, the "schwa" (upside

down "e," phonetically)
is the most common vowel sound.
If you properly shuffle a deck of cards, that deck
has never before been seen, *quidquid*
Latine dictum sit altum videtur
and exactly the same letters
can be found in silent and listen.

PILGRIMAGE

The location of one square inch of silence,
in the Hoh Rain Forest, marked
by a small red stone that rests atop
a moss-covered log. Hike about two
hours up from the Visitor's Center
above Mt. Tom Creek Meadows:
designated wilderness. I am unsure
if I have ever heard silence. I may have
issues with silence—its striations
of despair and solace, its love of control.
The path, limned with ferns, ancient trees,
is not hard. I believe we can manage.
And when we get there? (Shrug.)

FACE

One can achieve 97 percent neutrality
with three percent contempt.

In the Halls of Abstract Nouns, we all
have a bust like the potentates we are.

Though undignified to smile, I am trying
to reveal less. I become more mum and

see-through as I age. You would have
to ask what I was thinking. At best, at rest,

52 percent amused, 16 perplexed,
a single digit of wistfulness.

The remainder a mystery, even to me.

ACUSMATA

Pour libations to gods
from the ear of the cup;
don't craft their images
to wear on your fingers.
Make any sacrifice
barefoot. Put your right shoe
on first, eschew public
roads. Remember, planets
do not love you—they are
vehicles of divine
vengeance: only the moon
and sun can be trusted.
Marvel at silence, try
to be silent for five
years and if all else fails,
recall the *tetraktys*—
the first four numbers, which
when added together,
equal ten, the perfect
digits—the harmony,
believed Pythagoras
("chief of the charlatans,"
eye-rolled Heraclitus)
in which the Sirens sing.

ON DONNING A STATEMENT NECKLACE

I began to assert and
        assert, in a concatenate fashion.

Wheat chains, box chains, cable-link, snake chains, rope chains.
Figaro, Singapore, anchor.
Beaded and stoned, a pearl, a tooth, a locket, a cameo dangling.

      It takes over my
          neck and north chest,

rests on my clavicle, yearns toward cleavage. Inside, deep and superficial
muscles, bones and vessels, organs,
lymphatics—so complex, over-wrought—how the effort coordinates

      is beyond me and my
          many opinions.

As from a distance equaling rate times time, I hear my unmuttered
utterance, short
of stentorian though emphatic, and wonder if, before my death,

      I will turn quiet again, as when I was small
         and voiceless.

CURTAIN

There is no such thing as dream.
Only that life where the phrase "make sense"
has no meaning—as they say there,
if sense exists, it need not be made.
There are no modifiers there—no
wild night, no statement necklace, no
deep sadness. Each word a pillar.
Each word stands
on its own, alone, and true,
they are lonely. And strong.
Sometimes silent (that type).
No one owns them.
Last night I went there, thoroughly,
and was surprised at the story sutured
of person and event and place and death, you
were there, too, playing a bit part.

ACKNOWLEDGMENTS

"Coincidence." *Indicia*, Vol. 6.1, Summer/Fall 2023.

"Against Weltschmerz." *Posit*, 2022.

"What Flaubert Said." *Citric Acid*, Issue #4, 2022.

"Today's Flutter of Questions." *CCAR Journal: The Reform Jewish Quarterly*, Winter 2022.

"In my alternate reality." *Interlitq* 2020.

"Nocturne: Riffs." *Free Inquiry*, Volume 38, #4.

"As for this whole matter of happiness." *December*, 2017.

"Molly Picon Moment." "Time Certain." *Ghost Town*, 2017.

"The Important Parts." *Posit*, 2017.

"Morpho Peleides." *Third Coast*, Fall 2010.

"Wild One." *Askew*, 2009.

PATTY SEYBURN has previously published five collections of poems: *Threshold Delivery*, *Perfecta*, *Hilarity*, *Mechanical Cluster*, and *Diasporadic*. She was a Fulbright Scholar in Iasi, Romania and is a professor at California State University, Long Beach.

WHAT BOOKS PRESS

AN IMPRINT OF

THE GLASS TABLE

COLLECTIVE

LOS ANGELES

WHAT BOOKS feature cover art by Los Angeles painter, printmaker, muralist, and theater and performance artist GRONK. A founding member of ASCO, Gronk collaborates with the LA and Santa Fe Operas and the Kronos Quartet. His work is found in the Corcoran, Smithsonian, LACMA, and Riverside Art Museum's Cheech Marin collection.

As a small, independent press, we urge our readers to support independent publishers and booksellers. This is easily done by visiting our website, WhatBooksPress.com, where you can purchase books directly from us or from Bookshop.org

2017

*Gary Oldman Is a Building
You Must Walk Through*
FORREST ROTH
NOVEL

Rhombus and Oval
JESSICA SEQUEIRA
STORIES

Imperfect Pastorals
GAIL WRONSKY
POEMS

2016

The Mysterious Islands
A.W. DEANNUNTIS
STORIES

*The "She" Series:
A Venice Correspondence*
HOLADAY MASON
& SARAH MACLAY
POEMS

Mirage Industries
CAROLIE PARKER
POEMS

2015

*The Balloon Containing
the Water Containing the
Narrative Begins Leaking*
RICH IVES
STORIES

*The Shortest Farewells
Are the Best*
CHUCK ROSENTHAL
& GAIL WRONSKY
LITERARY COLLAGE/PROSE POEMS

2014

It Looks Worse Than I Am
LAURIE BLAUNER
POEMS

They Become Her
REBBECCA BROWN
NOVEL

*The Final Death of Rock-and-
Roll
& Other Stories*
A.W. DEANNUNTIS
STORIES

Perfecta
PATTY SEYBURN
POEMS

2013

Brittle Star
ROD VAL MOORE
NOVEL

Sex Libris
JUDITH TAYLOR
POEMS

Start With A Small Guitar
LYNNE THOMPSON
POEMS

Tomorrow You'll Be One of Us
GAIL WRONSKY,
CHUCK ROSENTHAL
& GRONK
ART/LITERARY COLLAGE/POEMS

WHAT BOOKS PRESS

LOS ANGELES

www.ingramcontent.com/pod-product-compliance
Lightning Source LLC
Chambersburg PA
CBHW031246120626
46545CB00007B/2678